The HUNCHBACK *of* NOTRE-DAME

Victor Hugo

JAICO PUBLISHING HOUSE

Ahmedabad Bangalore Chennai
Delhi Hyderabad Kolkata Mumbai

Published by Jaico Publishing House
A-2 Jash Chambers, 7-A Sir Phirozshah Mehta Road
Fort, Mumbai - 400 001
jaicopub@jaicobooks.com
www.jaicobooks.com

THE HUNCHBACK OF NOTRE-DAME
ISBN 978-93-88423-09-0

First Jaico Impression: 2019
Second Jaico Impression: 2022

Printed by
B.B. Press, Noida, U.P.

CONTENTS

Chapter 1

THE PALACE OF JUSTICE

It was the 6th of January, 1482. The people of Paris were awakened by a grand peal from all the bells in three districts of the Cite, the Universite, and the Ville. It was the day of the Festival of Fools. On that day there was to be an exhibition of fireworks in the Place de Greve, a may-tree planted at the chapel of Braque, and a mystery performed at the Palace of Justice.

All the avenues to the Palace of Justice were particularly crowded, because the Flemish ambassadors, who had arrived two days before, were going to attend the mystery (drama), and the election of the Pope of Fools.

It was the day of the Festival of Fools.

In the middle of the great hall of the palace, an enclosed platform lined with gold brocade, and to which a private entrance had been made, was erected specially for the Flemish envoys and other important guests.

The play was to be performed on the famous table, made out of a single piece of marble. Every eye was fixed on this table as the clock struck twelve. The crowd had been waiting since morning and its impatience was growing by every passing minute.

"The mystery! Begin the mystery at once!" shouted the crowd.

A tall and slender figure of a young man, who till now had stood silently near the marble table, came forward to address the actor, who had by now appeared on the platform.

"Begin immediately," he said to him. "I will pacify Monsieur the Bailiff and the Cardinal, for not waiting for their arrival."

The applaud that followed was absolutely deafening. The person, who had so magically

"The mystery! Begin the mystery at once!"

quietened the crowd, was Pierre Gringoire, the author of the mystery.

The first part of the play was hardly over

when a ragged beggar, perching himself just below the platform, began to drawl in a doleful tone and half closed eyes, "Charity, if you please!"

This was enough to distract the attention of the audience, who were already feeling bored because of the mystery.

It was further distracted by the sudden arrival of the Cardinal. All heads turned mechanically toward the enclosed platform. "The Cardinal! the Cardinal!" was the cry on every tongue, and the unlucky play was cut short for the second time.

The forty-eight ambassadors of the Maximilian of Austria, entered. The Cardinal then advanced with a low bow toward Guillaume Rym, councillor of the city of Ghent.

When all the distinguished guests had arrived, the play proceeded further once again.

"Charity, if you please".

But all of a sudden, Master Coppenole, the hosier of the city of Ghent, rose from his seat and addressed the crowd :

"Genglemen, if this is what you call a mystery", said he, "I must say it is not amusing. I came here to see the Festival of Fools. We have our Pope of Fools at Ghent too, but the say we do it is this—we collect a crowd, then, whoever wants, puts his head through a round space and grins at the crowd. The one who makes the ugliest face in chosen Pope. I assure you, it is a real entertainment. Shall we choose your Pope this way? At any rate, it will be more amusing than this play. We have ugly enough faces among us."

To Gringoire's utter horror, everything was ready in a moment to carry Coppenole's idea into effect. The little chapel opposite to the marble table was chosen for the scene of the grimaces. Coppenole supervised all the arrangements from his place. The Cardinal, in the meanwhile had left the hall, leaving the Flemings and Paris citizens to have their fun.

The grimaces began. Every ugly face was

'We have ugly enough faces among us.'

followed by loud shouts of laughter and stamping and clapping. The crowd was seized with a kind of fascination. Poor

Gringoire! He remained the only spectator of his play. Every back was turned on him.

Suddenly, there was a tremendous thunder of applause. The Pope of Fools was elected.

It was actually a miraculous ugliness, which absolutely dazzled the crowd. Master Coppenole himself applauded and Clopin Trouillefou, the beggar who had participated, admitted defeat.

The crowd rushed to the chapel and the lucky Pope of Fools was brought out. The crowd then realised that what had been mistaken for a grimace, was his natural expression. His enormous head was covered with red bristles. There was a large hump between his shoulders. His legs were a bow-shaped and feet and hands monstrous. He had a horse-shoe mouth and only one eye. But above all, his expression was a mixture of spite, wonder and melancholy.

He had a horse-shoe mouth and only one eye.

The crowd instantly recognized him and cried out in one voice, "It is Quasimodo, the hunchback of Notre-Dame! Quasimodo the bell-ringer! Hurrah! hurrah!"

Master Coppenole sportingly clapped his hand on the monster's shoulder. Qusimodo did not move, but there was a formidable air of strength, agility and courage about him.

"Why, you are the finest piece of ugliness I ever saw" said Coppenole. "You deserve to be Pope of Rome as well as Paris. What do you say?" Quasimodo made no reply.

An old woman informed Coppenole that Quasimodo was deaf.

"Deaf!" cried Coppenole. "He makes a perfect Pope of Fools."

"He talks when he wishes to," said the old woman.

"He became deaf with ringing the bells of Notre-Dame."

Meanwhile, the crowd had brought a pasteboard tiara and mock robe of the Pope of Fools. Quasimodo allowed these to be put upon him with a kind of proud docility. He

"Deaf! He makes a perfect Pope of Fools."

was then made to sit on a coloured litter, which was then carried on the shoulders of officers. The ragged procession then moved off, according to custom, through the galleries in the palace and then into the streets and public places of Paris.

A few spectators still lingered behind in the great hall.

"Well," thought Gringoire, "I can proceed with my mystery. Though their number is small, they are listening at any rate."

"Friends," suddenly one man in the window shouted, "it's La Esmeralda! La Esmeralda in the Place!"

This cry produced a magic effect. All those left in the hall ran to the windows, climbing over each other to have a better view, crying. "La Esmeralda! La Esmeralda!"

Gringoire was in despair. "What can they mean by La Esmeralda?" said he, "a pretty pack of asses, these Parisians! And what kind of word is it? It must surely be Egyptian."

"La Esmeralda! La Esmeralda!"

It was already dusk when Gringoire left the palace. He badly needed a good supper and a warm place to sleep in. Since he found it impossible to escape the rejoicing of the Pope of Fools, he decided to join the celebration. "At least" thought he "there will be a warming bonfire, and perhaps a supper."

When Pierre Gringoire reached the Place de Greve he was numbed with cold. He hurried toward the bonfire, around which a large crowd had gathered. In the space left between the fire and the crowd there was a young girl dancing.

Gringoire was absolutely fascinated by the dazzling beauty of the girl. She was not tall, but appeared so because of the gracefulness and slenderness of her figure. She was dark, but had a golden tint to her complexion. She danced, whirled around, on an old Persian carpet, and everytime she passed, Gringoire thought, her large, black eyes flashed lightning.

Every eye was fixed upon her. She was

She was dancing to the sound of a tambourine.

dancing along with the sound of a tambourine, her two plump, beautifully shaped arms held above her head. She was truly a supernatural being.

Among the thousand spectators, there was one man who seemed to be more deeply absorbed in the dancer than anyone else. This man looked calm and sombre. He appeared to be no more than thirty-five years of age, but he was nevertheless bald. His deep-sunk eyes were intently fixed on the Bohemian.

"Djali!" said the girl; and a little white goat started up. It had, till then, been lying at the corner of the carpet. "Djali, it is your turn now"; and, seating herself, she held the tambourine before the animal. She made Djali do many tricks, and the surprised spectators applauded.

"There is sorcery behind this" said the same bald man, who never took his eyes off the girl. The girl shuddered and turned away to collect the coins from the crowd in her tambourine. She came to Gringoire, who readily thrust his hand into his pocket, but

"There is sorcery behind this."

found nothing. The girl stood still before him, looking at him with her large eyes, and holding out her tambourine.

At that time the procession of the Pope of Fools, after parading through the main streets, was now entering the Place de Greve with all its noise and clamour. This procession was joined in its progress by all the vagabonds and thieves in Paris.

There was a peculiar expression of pride on Quasimodo's face as he saw beneath him, the heads of those straight, well-shaped men. Till now he had faced only disgust and humiliation for his ugliness. It did not matter to him that his subjects were a mob of thieves and cripples. This was the first time people had ever clapped for him. Behind this mock respect, however, there was a certain degree of real fear, for the hunchback was very strong.

When this procession was passing the crowd in the Place, a man suddenly darted from among the crowd, and with one swift angry movement, snatched the golden staff

There was a peculiar expression of pride on Quasimodo's face.

from Quasimodo's hands. This was the same bald man who had scared the poor gipsy girl.

The moment he had darted from among the crowd, Gringoire recognized him. "Why!" he cried in astonishment, "it s my master Dom Claudo Frollo, the Archdeacon. But what is he doing with that one-eyed monster?"

There were shrieks of terror from the crowd, as Quasimodo leaped from the litter to the ground. With one bound he was before the priest. Her looked at him and dropped upon his knees. The priest pulled off his tiara and broke his staff. Quasimodo remained still, bowing his head. Then they started a strange dialogue of signs and gestures. Neither of them spoke. The priest was erect, imperious, Quasimodo at his feet, humble and submissive. And yet Quasimodo could have crushed the priest in a moment.

Finally, the Archdeacon motioned Quasimodo to rise and follow him. The beggars and vagabonds were ready to defend their Pope, who had been so unceremoniously

They started a strange dialogue of signs and gestures.

dethroned. But Quasimodo, stepping before the priest, gritted his teeth like an angry tiger. He then went ahead, making way for the priest through the crowd. They went into a dark narrow street, and no one dared to follow them.

"It's really amazing!" exclaimed Gringoire," but where will I find my supper?"

Gringoire decided to follow the gipsy girl.

"After all," he thought, "she must be staying somewhere. She might give me something to eat."

The gipsy girl and her goat were a little ahead of him—two elegant, delicate and charming creatures. By this time, she had more than once turned her head and looked at him anxiously. This made Gringoire remain much behind her. On reaching a corner of a street where she had turned, he heard her piercing scream. The street was extremely dark and lonely; but Gringoire could see the Bohemian girl struggling between two men, who were trying to stifle her cries.

His one blow sent Grringoire reeling back.

Gringoire ran forward. One of the man turned upon him. It was Quasimodo. His one blow sent Gringoire reeling back. Then the hunchback turned and picked up the girl. His friend followed and the poor goat ran after three.

"Murder! Murder!" cried the gipsy girl.

"Stop, scoundrels, let her go!" suddenly roared a horseman who came dashing out of the next street, his sword in his hand. He snatched the girl out of grasp of Quasimodo and put her across his saddle. About ten armed soldiers had accompanied the horseman. Quasimodo was surrounded and captured. His friend had disappeared in the confusion.

The Bohemian girl gracefully raised herself and looked at her rescuer's handsome face. "What is your name, Sir?" she asked in a sweet tone.

"Captain Phoebus de Chateaupers, at your service, my dear," replied the officer.

"Thank you," said she and slid down the

"Captain Phoebus de Chateaupers, at your service, my dear"

horse's side to the ground, and vanished with the swiftness of lightning.

Chapter 2

THE BROKEN JUG

Gringoire, hurt by his fall, finally came to his senses. He thought of the violent scene which had just occurred. He recollected that Quasimodo had a companion; and the stately, morose figure of the Archdeacon vaguely came into his mind.

"But that is impossible," thought he.

Soon he realized he was freezing and lost in that dark night, and still without supper. He saw a dim light down a long narrow lane, which helped to cheer his spirits. But before reaching that light he found himself among strange people. One was a wretched cripple in a cart, the other also a cripple with crutches and the third was a little blind man with a long beard.

Gringoire finally came to his senses.

They came to an open square. Suddenly one cripple threw down his crutches, the other rose from his cart and the blind man stared Gringoire in the face with two flaming eyes.

"Where am I?" cried the frightened Gringoire. He cast his eyes around him. He was actually in the dreaded Cour des Miracles, where no honest man dared to enter in the night, where all the thieves and beggars who faked their injuries retired at night with their loot. It was a spacious area. Fires were blazing here and there. Strange looking groups had gathered around them. There was a bustle, confusion around Gringoire. He was grabbed by the three beggars.

"Lead him to the King!" they cried together.

"To the king! to the King" repeated every voice around him. He was hurried on. On a barrel near a fire sat the King—the same beggar who had disturbed Gringoire's play in the Palace.

He was grabbed by the three beggars.

Clopin Trouillefou held a whip in his hand. "You have entered our territory," said he. "Unless you are a thief, a beggar or a tramp, you will be punished."

"Alas!" sighed Gringoire, "I am an author."

"Enough!" cried the King. "You will be hanged."

"You cannot mean it! I am the same poet whose mystery was presented this morning in the great Palace."

"I was there too," said Clopin. "But tell me, because you annoyed us in the morning, is there any reason why you should not be hung now."

They put a crossbar across two poles and hung a rope from it. Gringoire was made to stand on a stool, with the rope round his neck.

"Wait a moment!" suddenly Clopin cried, "I forgot. This is your last chance. It is our custom not to hang anyone, till we ask the women if any of them will have you."

"Enough!" cried the King."
You will be hanged

He turned towards the woman: "Who will have a husband for nothing? Is there anyone among you who will marry this fellow? Come forward and see."

Gringoire, in this condition looked far from attractive, and none of the women showed any eagerness to accept the offer.

Suddenly a bright young girl stepped out of the crowd. Cries of "La Esmeralda! La Esmeralda!" arose among the vagabonds. Everybody respectfully drew back for her to pass. She watched Gringoire for a moment in silence.

"Are you going to hang this man?" she asked Clopin.

"Yes, sister," replied the King, "unless you will take him for your husband."

"I will take him," said she.

Gringoire was now convinced that he was in a dream. The noose was removed and he was brought down from the stool.

A clay jug was brought and the gipsy girl

"I will take him," said La Esmeralda.

handed it to him. "Drop it on the ground," said she to him. The jug broke into four pieces.

According to their custom it meant they were husband and wife for the next four years.

In a few moments Gringoire found himself with the gipsy girl in a small, warm room. The girl seemed to take no notice of him. As he came near her, she drew back. "What you want with me?" she inquired.

"What!" cried Gringoire, "am I not your husband?"

Suddenly she stooped and raised herself again with a little dagger in her hand. The little white goat also placed itself before her, in an attacking position.

"What a pair of crazy females!" said Gringoire. "But why did you take me for your husband?"

"Should I have let you be hanged?"

"Okay" sighed Gringoire, "I will not come to you without your permission. But for God's sake, give me something to eat."

Suddenly she stooped and raised herself again with a little dagger in her hand.

The Egyptian's dagger vanished and in a moment a loaf of bread, bacon, some apples and a jug of beer were set upon the table. Gringoire began to eat hungrily, while La Esmeralda sat before him engaged in some deep thought.

"If you do not love me," said Gringoire, "will you have me as a friend?"

"Perhaps," said she. "I don't even know your name."

"I am Pierre Gringoire," he began. "At six years of age, I was left without my parents. I grew up on streets, with whatever morsel of food was thrown to me. One day I met Dom Frollo, the Archdeacon of Notre-Dame who gave me shelter. It is because of him that today I am a learned man and an author."

Gringoire paused, waiting for her reaction.

"*Phoebus*," she turned to him—"What does that mean?"

"It is a Latin word," Gringoire replied; "it means the sun."

"The sun!" she exclaimed.

"The sun!" she exclaimed.

"It is also a name of a handsome archer, who was a god" added Gringoire.

Suddenly the girl and the goat slipped through the door. Before Gringoire could stop them, he heard the bolt of the door.

"At least she has left me a bed" sighed Gringoire. "It is of no use to complain, but this a strange wedding night!"

Chapter 3

NOTRE-DAME

The church of Notre-Dame is without doubt a sublime and majestic building. It is a vast symphony of stone, a genius of the artist, which shows in a hundred ways upon every stone. Its vastness strikes terror into the spectator. Every face of its statues, every stone of the structure is not only the history of France, but also the history of art and science.

A majestic view of Paris can be enjoyed from the top of the towers of Notre-Dame. You can reach the top after grouping your way up the dark spiral staircase, which lands abruptly on one of the two lofty platforms between the towers.

The Paris of the fifteenth century, was

The church of Notre-Dame—a majestic building.

already a gigantic city. You could get a bird's eye view of the three towns of Paris—the Cite, the Universite, and the Ville. The Seine river runs across these three parts.

Chapter 4

THE FOUNDLING

Sixteen years before this period, one fine morning, a living creature of four years of age was found after the Mass in the church of Notre-Dame, in the wooden bed in the porch. It was customary to expose foundlings to the public charity. A number of old women had collected round it. They were observing the creature out of curiosity.

"Is that the way they make children nowadays?" inquired one old woman.

"It must be a sin to look at that thing" rejoined another.

"It's a miracle!" exclaimed the third one.

This "little miracle" as they called it, was a shapeless, moving thing, tied up in its bed,

A number of old women had collected round it.

only its head exposed. And that head was absolutely hideous. The monstrous creature

"I adopt this child," said the priest.

was struggling in its sack, and the crowd was increasing around.

For some time, a young priest had been

listening to the comments of the old women. He was a man of sombre presence and piercing eyes. Without speaking, he pushed aside the crowd and examined 'the little monster'. He took him in his hands.

"I adopt this child," said the priest.

As the onlookers watched with horror, he wrapped him and carried him away, and in a few moments was out of sight.

"Didn't I tell you," cried one of the old women to her companion, "that young clerk, Monsieur Claude Frollo, is a sorcerer."

Chapter 5

THE BELL-RINGER OF NOTRE-DAME

Claude Frollo, in fact, was no ordinary person. He came from one of the prestigious families of Paris. From his childhood his parents sent him to the Church. He soon became a learned young scholar.

When he was nineteen, he lost his parents. They left only an infant brother for Claude Frollo. He gave all his life to raise this infant brother, bestowing on him all the possible care and attention.

This mixture of learning and humility, so uncommon at his age, quickly gained him the admiration and the respect of the convent. At the age of twenty, he became a

He soon became a learned young man.

priest. His reputation for learning spread among the people; some of them even

The statues of saints and monsters were his friends.

thought him a sorcerer—a common bias in that superstitious age.

It was at this time that he came across the little creature which was left in Notre-Dame. His heart melted with pity, when he took the hideous child in his arms. He baptized this child and named him Quasimodo; for, the day he was found, happened to be Quasimodo Sunday.

The poor little wretch was a monster of deformity. He had a big wart over his left eye, his head was close to his shoulders, his back arched, his breast-bone protruded, and his legs twisted. But he appeared lively and healthy. His extreme ugliness only helped to increase the compassion of Claude. He vowed in his heart to bring up this boy for the love of his own brother.

Notre-Dame became Quasimode's home, his country, his world. He knew and loved every inch of it. The statues of saints and monsters were his friends. He climbed its towers like a mountain goat. But most of all he loved the great bells of the church. With great difficulty and patience Claude Frollo had taught him to speak. But having become bell-ringer of Notre Dame at the age of fourteen, the volume of sound made him deaf. Because of his deafness, he became somewhat dumb also. He was mischievous. His strength was developed in the most extraordinary manner. As he grew up, he found only hatred about him. Because of this rejection, his cathedral was enough for him.

This extraordinary being seemed to give the whole cathedral a breath of life. His presence was felt everywhere. He was the soul of gigantic building.

The only human being whom Quasimodo loved as much or even more than his cathedral was Claude Frollo-who had raised him, protected him and made him the bell-ringer. To please Claude Frollo, he would have thrown himself from the top of the towers of Notre-Dame.

He became more and more gloomy as a man

In 1482, Quasimodo was about twenty years of age and Calude Frollo about thirty six. Claude Frollo was now Archdeacon. He

His hatred for Egyptians and Bohemians seemed to have become more violent.

was an aweinspiring person before whom the singing boys and clerks in Notre-Dame trembled with fear. He became more and more learned, but at the same time, more and more rigid as a priest and more and more gloomy as a man.

The Archdeacon had fixed up a secret cell for himself, at the top of the tower, nearest to the Greve. It was said that no one but the Bishop dared enter this cell without his permission. No one knew what that cell contained. But these facts helped to form that formidable reputation about the Archdeacon.

He had always kept aloof from women; now he seemed to dislike them more than ever. His hatred for Egyptians and Bohemians seemed to have become more violent. He had expressly prohibited the Bohemians to come and dance in the area of the church. He had recently searched through the archives for cases of wizards and witches sentenced to the gallows for practising the black art in association with cats, swine, or goats.

Now let us return to our story.

"Are you making fun of me?"

The day after Festival of Fools, Quasimodo was brought into court. He was bound and surrounded by guards. Quasimodo was silent.

From time to time, he merely glanced angrily at the bonds which confined him.

"Quasimodo," began the judge, "You are accused of attacking a woman, and of fighting the members of the guard. Do you have anything to say?"

The poor devil, thinking that the judge was asking his name, replied in a harsh, guttural voice, "Quasimodo."

At this, the onlookers burst into laughter. The judge, flushed with rage, exclaimed :

"Are you making fun of me?"

"Bell-ringer at Notre-Dame," replied Quasimodo, thinking that the judge inquired his profession.

"Bell ringer!" roared the judge. "How dare you answer me without respect? Take this fellow to the pillory at once and let him be whipped for a whole hour. Further, keep him there for another hour as additional punishment."

Chapter 6

THE PILLORY

In the Place de Greve, four sergeants were posted at the four corners of the pillory which consisted of a cube of masonry about ten feet high. A flight of steps of rough stone led to the upper platform, upon which there was a wheel. The culprit was bound upon this wheel, kneeling, and with his hands tied behind him. An axle of timber caused the wheel to revolve, and thus exhibited the culprit's face to every point of the Place. This was called 'turning' a criminal.

Quasimodo was tied to a cart and brought upto the pillory. He was hoisted upon the platform among loud cheers and laughter. It was strange to be treated in this manner by

He was hoisted upon the platform among loud cheers and laughter.

the same mob, who on the previous day had proclaimed him the Pope of Fools.

The thin lashes descended with fury upon the back of the culprit.

He was placed on his knees on the circular floor and his shirt was taken off.

Quasimodo never uttered a word. There was no emotion on his face other than astonishment of an idiot.

A loud laugh burst forth from the mob as Quasimodo's naked hump and camel breast were visible. Amid this laughter, a man climbed the steps to the platform, carrying a whip of long white thongs. The first thing he did was to set down an hour-glass, the upper division of which was full of red sand, that dropped into the lower half. With his left hand, he carelessly turned up the right sleeve of his shirt and stamped his foot. The wheel began to turn.

Quasimodo shook all over. The amazement suddenly expressed on his hideous face drew shouts of laughter.

At the moment when the turning wheel presented the huge shoulders of Quasimodo, the torturer raised his arm. The thin lashes descended with fury upon the back of the

Quasimodo's eye slowly opened.

culprit. Quasimodo started like one awakened from a dream, and struggled in his bonds. He had begun to comprehend the meaning of the scene. The wheel continued to turn and the whip continued to fall. Blood began to trickle in a hundred little streams down the shoulders of the hunchback, but not a single sigh came from him.

He first tried to break his bonds. His eye was seen to flash and his muscles swelled. The effort was mighty and desperate, but, in vain. Then he closed his only eye, dropped his head upon his breast and waited without stirring.

At last, the torturer stopped; the wheel stopped, and Quasimodo's eye slowly opened.

Two attendants washed the bleeding back of the sufferer, rubbed some ointment on it, which in a short time closed all the wounds.

Quasimodo's punishment was not yet over. He had still to remain in the pillory another hour. The hour-glass was again turned, and Quasimodo was left bound as before.

Slowly a cloud of rage, hatred and despair spread over that hideous face.

The hunchback was generally hated by the public. His appearance at the pillory had excited a universal joy. The severe punishment given to him, and the pitiful condition in which it had left him; far from softening the crowd, had rendered its hatred more strong.

Quasimodo was deaf, but he was sharp-sighted. He glared at the crowd that laughed and threw stones at him. He then struggled in his bonds, which made the old wheel of the pillary creak. This served only to increase the jeers of the crowd. Quasimodo again became quiet. But slowly a cloud of rage, hatred and despair spread over that hideous face.

For a moment, however, the face of the poor creature assumed a look of gentleness. He caught a glimpse of a priest in the distance. As the priest approached, a gentle smile spread over his coarse features. But the moment the priest recognised the hunchback, he cast down his eyes, and went away as if in a hurry. This priest was the Archdeacon, Claude Frollo.

Quasimodo's expression became darker than ever. The smile lingered, mixed with bitterness and disappointment. He was exposed to the public hatred for almost one and a half hour now. Suddenly, breaking his silence, he cried in a hoarse and furious voice like a wild beast "Water!"

This cry only made the crowd laugh louder.

"Take that to drink your water from!" shouted a fellow, throwing at him a broken jug, which hit him upon his chest.

"Water!" roared the panting Quasimodo, again.

At that moment, he saw the crowd making way for a young female who was coming to the pillory. She was followed by a little white goat. Quasimodo recognized her. It was the Bohemian girl whom he had tried

She gently lifted a cup of water of Quasimodo's parched lips.

to carry off the previous night. In his confusion, he thought she was coming to punish him and vainly tried to avoid her. Without uttering a word, she came to the hunchback, and gently lifted a cup of water to his parched lips.

There was a big tear in the hunchback's bloodshot eye. He drank the water greedily. The crowd shouted and cheered. "Hurrah! Hurrah!" On a pillory this sight was a sublime. The crowd was moved by it. Among loud clapping and shouting La Esmeralda came down from the pillory.

Chapter 7

THE GIRL AND HER GOAT

Several weeks had passed. It was now the beginning of March.

Opposite to the lofty cathedral of Notre-Dame, over the porch of a rich Gothic building, some young, rich ladies were chatting merrily with a handsome young captain in uniform.

Apparently the Captain was engaged to Fleurde-Lys in whose apartment they were gathered. But it was evident from his cold and absent manner that he was not very happy with the match.

At this moment, a young girl in the group, looking down upon the Place, cried : "Oh, look at that pretty dancer on the pavement, playing on a tambourine."

The Captain was not very happy with the match.

"Some Egyptian," replied Fleur-de-Lys in a careless manner. The Captain, relieved by this interruption which cut short a highly tiring conversation, gladly joined the group in the balcony.

"Isn't she the same Bohemian," Flour-de-Lys asked suddenly, "whom you rescued about two months back?"

"Yes, I think I know her by her goat" replied the Captain.

"Oh! what a pretty little goat," exclaimed the young girl, clapping her hands.

"See," she began again, "who is that man up there?"

All the young ladies looked up. A man was indeed standing on the topmost balustrade of the northern tower of Notre-Dame overlooking the Greve. It was the priest, Claude Frollo, as his dress was clearly visible. His head was supported by both his hands, and he was as motionless as a statue.

"It's the Archdeacon!" exclaimed the young girl "how he looks at the dancing girl."

"Isn't she the same Bohemian whom you rescued about two months back?"

"Let the gipsy girl beware," said Fleur-de-Lys. The Archdeacon is not fond of gipsies."

Then turning the captain she said, "Phoebus, since you know this girl, why not call her up. She will amuse us."

"I don't even know her name," said Phoebus. "However, if you wish, I will call her."

Phoebus called La Esmeralda. She paused in her dancing and looked up. She then blushed deeply and made her way through the circle of spectators toward the large house.

A moment later, the Bohemian appeared at the door of the apartment, out of breath, with her large eyes fixed on the floor. Her beauty was so surpassing, that, in spite of themselves, the young ladies were dazzled.

They received her very coldly. They surveyed her from head to foot. The Captain spoke first :

"Come in my dear" said he, "do you remember me?"

"Come in my dear," said the Captain.

"Oh, yes" said she, as she looked up at him.

"Why did you run away that night? did I scare you?"

"Oh, no!" cried the girl.

"What a lovely girl," remarked Phoebus.

"But very poorly dressed" said one young lady.

"Does she run about the streets in that short skirt?" asked another.

"My dear," Fleur-de-Lys said, " If you cover your arms decently, they would not be so sunburnt."

They seemed to take no account of her presence and talked about her as if she was an object.

The Bohemian stood motionless, fixing a troubled but gentle look upon Phoebus.

"Oh! here is the pretty little goat with golden feet" cried the young girl with joy." I have heard that her goat performs the most amazing tricks."

"Child, make your goat perform a miracle for us."

"Child" said one young lady, "make your goat perform a miracle for us."

"I do not know what you mean," said the gipsy.

"Girl, if you or your goat are not going to amuse us, you can leave," said Fleur-de-Lys angrily.

"Oh, no!" exclaimed Phoebus, "you will not go so soon. By the way, what is your name my pretty dear?"

"La Esmeralda," said the Bohemian.

At this strange name the young ladies burst into a loud laughter.

"A terrible name that, for a girl," observed one lady.

Meanwhile the young child had loosened a little bag, which was hanging from the goat's neck, and emptied its contents on the mat. They consisted of some separate little alphabets in wood. At once, the goat sorted out some letters with her golden foot, shuffled them gently together and arranged

"Come and see what the goat has done."

them in a particular order. The young girl, clapping her hands cried : "Come and see what the goat has done!"

Everyone hastened to the spot. What they saw really made them cry out in surprise. The letters which the goat had arranged on the floor formed the name 'Phoebus'. la Esmeralda began to tremble as if she had committed a crime, and the Captain stared at her with admiration.

Suddenly La Esmeralda picked up the letters, made a sign to her Djali and left.

Captain Phoebus, after hesitating for a moment, followed her.

The priest, whom the young ladies had observed on the top of the north tower of Notre-Dame, was in fact the Archdeacon Claude Frollo.

Every day, before sunset, the Archdeacon climbed up the staircase of the tower and shut himself in his cell, where he frequently passed whole nights. On this day, just as he had reached the door of his cell, he heard the sounds of a tambourine. These sounds came from the Place du Parvis. The next moment

It was a fixed look, which flashed fire.

he was on top of the tower, looking intently at the dancing Bohemian. It would have been difficult to decide the nature of that look. It was a fixed look, which flashed fire.

Suddenly he was a man dressed in a yellow and red loose coat, who seemed to be that companion of the Bohemian. "Who is that man?" muttered the Archdeacon; "till now I have always seen her alone."

In a few minutes, Claude Frollo descended the staircase and mingled with the crowd which had gathered around the dancing girl. Instead of the Bohemian, who was dancing on the carpet a few moments before, the man in the yellow and red coat was sitting. The Archdeacon, having recognised the man, went to him immediately.

"What are you doing here Pierre Gringoire?" he asked, "How come you are now in the dancing girl's company?"

"Because she is my wife, Master," replied Gringoire.

"What are you talking about?" The priest's eyes glared like fire.

Gringoire related to him the story of his marriage to La Esmeralda, and also told him

The priest's eyes glowed like fire.

how the girl, to his day had not allowed him to touch her. He said though he was deeply in love with the Bohemian, he loved her goat almost as dearly. It was a charming, gentle and intelligent creature. The sorceries of the goat were, however, mere innocent tricks,. These Gringoire explained to the Archdeacon, who appeared to be very much interested. It was enough, he said, to hold the tambourine to the animal in such a way, to make it do what you wished. The girl had taken only two months to teach the goat to put together movable letters to form the word 'Phoebus'.

"Why Phoebus?" exclaimed the Archdeacon.

"God knows," replied Gringoire. "She frequently repeats it to herself, when she thinks she is alone."

"Are you sure" asked the Archdeacon "that it is only a word, not a name?"

"I do not know, Master," replied Gringoire. "But Master, tell me how does all this concern you?"

The Archdeacon's face crimsoned like that of a girl. "Listen, Gringoire" said he, "I take interest for your welfare. Let me tell you, the moment you but touch this Egyptian,

"The moment you but touch this Egyptian, calamity will fall upon you."

that child of the devil, calamity, will fall upon you. That is all I have to say." With this he retreated hurriedly beneath the gloomy arcades of the cathedral.

Chapter 8

THE GOBLIN-MONK

Several evenings later, on a dark night, two friends—one of them Captain Phoebus—left the tavern where the two were drinking together.

As the corner of a street the sound of a tambourine was heard. "That Bohemian should not see me here in this street," said Phoebus, walking hurriedly.

"What Bohemian?" asked the friend.

"That girl with the goat."

"La Esmeralda?"

"The same one, But I always forget her name. I am going to meet her tonight," Phoebus boasted.

"I am going to meet her tonight."

"Are you sure she will come?" asked the friend.

"Don't be silly" said Phoebus smiling, "I am very much sure."

"Captain Phoebus, you are a lucky fellow," said the friend.

Nearby in the shadow, a hooded figure watched and listened.

When the friend left, Phoebus walked on alone. Suddenly, he saw a kind of shadow creeping behind him along the walls. When he stopped, the figure also stopped, when he walked on, the figure also walked on.

Phoebus was not greatly alarmed. "After all," he muttered, "I have not a single farthing on me."

The street was absolutely deserted. Nothing was to be seen but the figure in cloak and hood. When very near to him, it stopped and remained motionless as a statue, fixing its eyes on him.

The Captain was a brave man. But this strange figure filled him with horror. At that

This strange figure filled the Captain with horror.

time, there were a number of stories of a goblin monk who haunted the streets of Paris at night.

The figure grasped the arms to Phoebus forcefully "Captain Phoebus" said he at the same moment.

"What the devil!" cried Phoebus, "How do you know my name?"

"You are going to meet a girl," said the figure.

"Oh, yes," answered the surprised Phoebus. "A girl named La Esmeralda."

"Captain Phoebus, you lie."

"How dare you say that," cried the Captain, drawing his sword; "Draw you sword, this very moment. It should decide who is lying."

The man neither flinched nor stirred. "Some other time Captain,' said he, "You forget your engagement."

"In fact," said Phoebus, keeping back the sword "a sword and a girl are always two delightful things to encounter in a meeting."

"How dare you say that," cried the Captain, drawing his sword.

"No, go to your meeting first," reminded the stranger.

"Thanks, sir, for your courtesy" said Phoebus. Then, "Oh, I forgot, I must have some money and I have not a single coin left."

"Here it is," said the stranger, at the same time slipping money in Phoebus hand.

"By heaven!" he exclaimed, "you are a good fellow."

"One condition," said the stranger, "you must take me with you. I will hide in some corner from where I will be able to tell whether the girl is really the same one you mentioned."

"That will make no difference to me," replied Phoebus carelessly.

They walked away hurriedly and in a few minutes came on the river tank, near Pont Saint-Michael, which was covered with small houses. Phobus stopped before a low door and knocked loudly. The door was instantly

The Captain's companion drew his cloak to his eyes.

opened by a very old woman, who held a lamp in her hand.

After entering the house, the Captain's companion drew his cloak up to his eyes. Phoebus put into the hand of the old woman the coin which had been given to him by the stranger. The old woman asked both of them to follow her and they ascended a ladder. On reaching the room above, Phoebus opened a door that led to a dark closet.

"This way, my friend" said he to his companion. The man in the cloak complied without uttering a word. The door closed upon him, and he heard Phoebus go downstairs with the old woman. The light disappeared along with them.

Claude Frollo—for he was the hooded companion of Phoebus—groped about for a few moments in the darkness. The room had neither a window nor a loophole and Claude Frollo had to crouch in the dust because of the inclined roof.

Suddenly the stairs creaked and the door

She kept looking at her own fingers, while the Captain looked at her with delight.

opened. From the small slit in the door the Archdeacon could see the room below. The old woman entered first, with the lamp in her hand, then Phoebus, and then, a third face; the beautiful and graceful face of Esmeralda.

Soon, Phoebus and Esmeralda were alone, sitting on the wooden stool beside the lamp. Because of the light of the lamp, the priest could see their two youthful faces clearly.

The girl was flushed and confused. She kept looking at her own fingers, while the Captain looked at her with delight.

"Oh, please do not hate me," she said without raising her eyes, "But, I think what I am doing is wrong."

"Hate you, my dear!" exclaimed Phoebus; "but why?"

La Esmeralda was silent for a moment. A tear trickled from her eye, "Oh, Phoebus, I love you!" she said.

This confession made Phoebus bolder. He threw his arms around La Esmeralda.

"Teach me your religion."

Gently removing his hands, she continued; "You have saved me. Who am I but a poor orphan! It was you that I dreamt of before

I knew you. Do you love me Phoebus?"

"Do I love you, angel?" exclaimed the Captain, sinking on his knees, "I love you and never loved anyone but you."

Suddenly she turned towards him. "Phoebus," said she, her eyes filled with love, "Teach me your religion."

"My religion!" cried the Captain, bursting into a laugh; "what do you want with my religion?"

"So that we may be married," replied the girl.

"What should we marry for?" Surprise showed on his face.

The girl turned pale, and sadly bowed her head.

"My dear girl" he resumed softly, "what is the use of marriage? These are all silly notions."

Dom Claude was watching all that passed.

She saw the dagger descending upon the Captain!

He was quivering and boiling with rage. He looked like a tiger looking through his cage.

The Captain was still talking sweetly to

her when the priest saw the girl throwing her arms around Phoebus.

Suddenly, above the head of the Captain she saw another head, and close to this face a hand holding a dagger. The girl recognised this face. She could not even scream in her fright. She saw the dagger descending upon the Captain and she fainted.

When she came to herself, she was surrounded by soldiers. The Captain was carried away bathed in blood. The priest had disappeared. The window at the farther end of the room, which looked toward the river was wide open. She heard the men saying to one another; "The sorceress has stabbed the captain."

Chapter 9

THE TRIAL

It was now over a month. Gringoire and other vagabonds were extremely worried—La Esmeralda was missing. One night the girl and her goat had disappeared and all the search had proved useless.

One day, when Gringoire was passing the Tournelle, a prison for criminals, he saw a crowd at the door of the Palace of Justice.

"What is going on here?" he asked one of the men.

"It seems that a woman is on trial for murdering an officer of the King's Ordnance. There seems to be sorcery behind this, so the Bishop as well the Archdeacon have also taken keen interest in the case."

"It seems that a woman is on trial for murdering an officer of the King's Ordnance.

Upon hearing the Archdeacon's name, Gringoire followed the crowd inside the

"I could only see his eyes which quite frightened me."

Palace. The hall was spacious and dark. The tall windows admitted only a faint light.

To his horror Gringoire found that La Esmeralda was standing in the middle of the court. It was she they were trying in this murder case. And old woman was under examination as an important witness.

"Gentlemen," she said "it is true that I have a house at the Pont Saint-Michael. One night while I was spinning, there was a knock at my door. When I opened it two men came in. One was a handsome officer. The other man was in black cloak and hat and I could only see his eyes, which quite frightened me. They gave me a crown and asked to lead them to my room upstairs, which is my best room. We went upstairs and while my back was turned the man in black was gone. I was a bit surprised. The officer went downstairs with me and then went out. He then returned again with a pretty girl of about sixteen years of age. She had a large goat with her and I must say

"Phoebus!" cried the girl, "where is he?"

that goat really disturbed me. I don't like those animals. They smell of witchcraft.

"Well, they went to the room upstairs and

I resumed my spinning. Suddenly I heard a scream upstairs and something fell upon the floor and the window opened. From my window I saw a black figure jumping out and tumbling into the river. It was a ghost dressed as a priest. I saw it swimming away towards the city. I immediately called the guards. When we went up, my best room was drenched with blood. The Captain, lying on the floor with a dagger in his bosom; and the girl pretending to be dead. 'Well' I said to myself,' it will take me long to clean my floor.' They carried away the poor young man and the girl with her goat."

The old woman stopped speaking. A murmur arose from the hall.

"The ghost, the goat and everything look like sorcery" everyone was saying.

"Phoebus!' suddenly the girl cried," where is he? Oh, please, for mercy's sake tell if he is alive."

"Silence" said the judge harshly. "We have nothing to do with that. And now bring in the second prisoner."

All eyes turned towards a small door which opened and in walked a pretty goat. She came in and nestled gracefully at the feet of her mistress. In those days it was common to find animals guilty of witchcraft.

The King's Proctor held the tambourine in a particular way to the goat, and asked "What hour is it?"

The goat raised her gilt foot and struck seven strokes. It was actually seven o'clock. Djali was made to perform some more tricks and everyone, except La Esmeralda and Grigoire, was convinced that the goat had the devil in it.

The judge, in a solemn tone, spoke; "Girl, you, with the devil's goat, stabbed and killed Captain Phoebus. Do you deny this?"

"I deny it" said she in a fearful tone; "It

was a priest, a priest in a cloak, who follows me."

"I order that she be tortured until she confesses" said the judge.

The poor girl was made to walk towards a low door, which closed after she went in. Shaking all over, La Esmeralda was led down a long corridor into a frightening dark cell. In this cell there were a variety of instruments of torture lying all over. The "sworn torturer" was standing there along with his two assistants. At one corner, there was a table at which a clerk sat with pen, ink paper.

"My dear girl," one of the men said : "do you still deny the charge?"

"Yes." she replied in a faint voice.

"Well, in that case, please be seated on this bed." He pointed towards a bed.

La Esmeralda remained standing, bewildered.

"I order that she be tortured until she confesses."

"What shall we begin with?" the man asked the torturer.

"The boot."

Suddenly she found herself seated on the strange looking bed. An iron-bound wooden boot was placed around her small foot. A screw was tightened. The boot became more and more contracted. At that first pain she screamed.

"Stop!—do you confess?" asked the man.

"Everything!" cried the girl. "I confess everything!"

"Clerk, write," ordered the Kings servant.

"Esmeralda, you confess your part in the witchcraft and sorcery?"

"Yes." Her voice was scarcely heard.

When she again entered the Court, pale and trembling, she was greeted with great pleasure. It was now dark and everyone wanted the business to be over as soon as possible.

"I confess everything."

It was declared that the accused had confessed the crime.

"You should know" said the Judge

"Only put me to death soon."

solemnly, "that even if you confess, you should expect only death."

"Whatever you please" said the girl in a broken voice, "Only put me to death soon."

She heard a chilling voice pronounce : "You shall be drawn in a cart, barefoot, to the Church of Notre Dame, and there, confess your sins to a priest; then taken to the Place de Greve and hanged. And likewise your goat."

Chapter 10

THE MEETING

She was thrown into a dark cell. In those days when a building was complete, there was almost as much of it underground as above. A palace, a fortress, a church had always a double basement. At the Bastille Saint-Antoine, at the Palace of Justice, these underground floors were prisons. The stories of these prisons became more and more contracted and gloomy. Once a prisoner was thus pushed in these cells, there was no light, no air and no life. La Esmeralda was thrust in—for fear that she might escape—with the mighty Palace of Justice over her head.

There she was surrounded by darkness and silence, crouched on a little straw, in the

She was surrounded by darkness and silence.

pool formed by water that dripped from the walls of her cell—What more could she suffer? How long she had been in this place she did not know. She did try to count the minutes measured by the drop of water; but then her mind discontinued this task, and left her in a state of shock.

One day, however, she heard a faint noise at the door of her cell. She raised her head and saw a reddish ray entering from the trapdoor. At the same time, the heavy ironbars rattled and the door turned. She saw a figure, but the door was too low to look as its head. The sudden light was so painful that she closed her eyes.

When she opened them again, the door was shut, a lantern was placed on one of the steps and someone stood before her. He wore a black wrapper and a hood concealed the face. For some time she kept her eyes fixed intently on this figure. Nobody spoke.

At last she asked : "Who are you?"

"A priest." The voice made her shudder.

He wore a black wrapper and a hood concealed the face.

"Are you prepared to die?" asked the priest in a low tone, "It will be tomorrow."

"Why such a long time?" she murmured, "why not today?"

"You must be very unhappy" the priest seemed to look around in the cell. "Without light, without fire, in the water. It is horrible."

"I am very cold," She answered, clasping her feet with her hands. Suddenly, she burst out crying like a child : "I want to leave this place, Sir, I am afraid. And there are horrible things which crawl upon me."

"Then come along with me." the priest took hold of her arm. His hand was very cold.

"Who are you?" she whispered.

The priest pushed back his hood. She looked at him. It was the same sinister face which had haunted her. The same face of the Archdeacon, whom she had last seen above the head of her dear Phoebus, with a dagger.

"It is the priest!" she cried, holding her hands over her eyes.

It was the same sinister face which had haunted her.

"Are you afraid of me?" he asked.

"Yes," said she, sobbing; "for months you

have been haunting, terrifying me. You have killed my Phoebus. What have I done to you? Why should you hate me so?"

"I love you," said the priest.

Her tears suddenly stopped. She stared at him vacantly.

"Oh, what love," she exclaimed shuddering. "The love of one who will burn in hell."

Both remained silent for some minutes.

"Listen," said the priest, "You will know all. Before I saw you I was happy. But from the day I saw you dancing, I was crazy. I followed you, I watched you and each day I loved you more. You possess that super human beauty that can come only from heaven. You were an angel. But then I saw a goat near you, an animal which is associated with witches: Then I had no further doubt that you had come from hell, to destroy me."

"You possess that super-human beauty that can come only from heaven."

The priest stopped, and then coldly added. "I still believe so."

There was another pause and then he continued.

"I was always following you. I had the idea of carrying you off. We almost had you in our arms, when that officer came up and save you."

"Oh! my Phoebus" said the girl softly.

"Not that name," cried the priest, seizing her arm fiercely. "It is that name which has ruined us. You are suffering, you know it. But you do not know how I have suffered. You do not know what unhappiness is. To love a woman, to be a priest, to be hated, to see her waste her love on a silly fool."

"Oh! my Phoebus," were the only words the girl uttered.

"Have pity on me, girl." The priest was on his knees. "I beg you not to hate me. I love you. I am miserable. But we could still be happy. I could help you escape. The place where you are will be a paradise to me."

She lunged at him like a tigress.

She just stared at him fixedly. "What has happened to my Phoebus?" she asked.

"Ah!" cried the priest, loosing her arm

from his grasp, "You have no pity."

"What has happened to Phoebus" she repeated coldly.

"He is dead" replied the priest.

"Then why ask me to live," she said. Suddenly she lunged at him like a tigress, "Go away, murderer! Leave me to die. Be yours, Priest! Never! Never! Noting will bring us together, not even hell itself !"

Slowly, Claude Frollo began to climb the steps, picking up his lantern. The girl stared after him. Suddenly he turned at the door. His face was horrible.

"I tell you, he is dead." With this he went out. Esmeralda fell with her face to the ground, and once more no sound was heard in the cell, other than that of the dripping water.

Phoebus, meanwhile, was not dead. When the Archdeacon said to the girl, "He is dead"

Esmeralda fell with her face to the ground.

he simply knew nothing about the matter. Though badly wounded, he had recovered. The injury was less serious than the

Archdeacon thought. This fact, however, had not affected the judicial proceedings. In those days, justice cared little about facts in a criminal case. All they cared about was the hanging of the accused. The judge believed that Phoebus was dead, and that was quite enough.

Phoebus had just joined his company, a few miles away from Paris. He felt that he would be ridiculed, if he took any part in this affair at this stage. In fact he could not tell what to make out of this affair and was eager to forget the whole thing.

One fine morning, two months after the stabbing, he came again to call upon the lady who lived opposite Notre-Dame.

"Ah, Phoebus," Fleur-de-Lys greeted him, "where have you been for these two months?"

Phoebus was embarrassed, "Why...our duty...besides, I was wounded."

There was an immense crowd waiting for a sinister spectacle.

"Wounded!" the girl exclaimed.

"Oh, you need not worry. It was a small

thing. But!" he cried in order to change the topic, "Look, what a crowd there is in the Place."

"Yes" replied the girl as they both came on the balcony, "I heard that a witch is to do penance this morning before the church and then to be hung afterwards."

In the Place du Parvis, in front of Notre-Dame there was an immense crowd, waiting for a sinister spectacle. At this moment the clock of Notre-Dame struck twelve. One big shout of "There she is" burst from pavement, windows and roofs.

A cart, drawn, and completely surrounded by horsemen had just entered the Place. Beside the cart, rode some officers of justice and police. In the cart was seated a young girl, her hands tied behind her. She was stripped to her chemise. Her long black hair fell loosely over her half covered shoulders. Through this flowing hair, a grey, knotty

The cart stopped before the central porch.

cord could be seen around the white, delicate skin of the girl's neck. At her feet there was a little goat, also bound.

"Look," said Fleur-de-Lys sharply to the Captain, "It is that Bohemian girl with her goat."

"I..what Bohemian?" stammered Phoebus.

"Are you shocked to see that gipsy?" asked the lady suspiciously.

"Me! not at all" said he with a forced grin.

"Then stay here with me and watch."

Meanwhile the cart had now reached the Parvis. Many from the crowd, on seeing her so beautiful and helpless, were moved with pity.

The cart stopped before the central porch. The great doors of the church opened, and there burst from the church a grave, loud and monotonous chant, sung by aged men.

The girl's hands were unbound, and she was then made to walk barefoot on the steps leading to the porch.

The chanting in the church stopped. In a

"Will you be mine? I can still save you."

few moments a long procession of priests and deacons slowly advanced towards the girl. But her eyes were fixed on him who walked at the head of the procession. "Oh!" she whispered to herself, shuddering, "there he is again! The priest."

The Archdeacon advanced, chanting with a loud voice. When he appeared in the broad day light outside the church, he looked as pale and white as a marble statue.

The Archdeacon approached her slowly. He addressed her in a loud voice, "Bohemian girl, have you prayed to God to pardon your crimes?" Then stooping, as if to receive her last confession, he whispered, "Will you be mine? I can still save you."

She stared at him fiercely, "Go to the devil, or I will expose you."

"They will not believe you," he grinned cruelly.

"What have you done to my Phoebus?"

At that moment the priest raised his head and saw Phoebus on the balcony, with the

"Phoebus!" she cried wildly, "you are alive."

lady. He shuddered, and there was a violent expression on his face.

"Well then, die!" said he. "No one will have you."

He turned his back on the prisoner and joined the priests, and then they disappeared in the church.

The unfortunate girl started going to the cart, to start her last journey. At that moment she raised her eye towards heaven. Suddenly she gave a loud scream; a scream of joy. In the balcony at the corner of the Place she saw Phoebus, just as he looked when they had met.

"Phoebus!" she cried, "my Phoebus!"

But then she saw the Captain knit his brow, say a few words to the young lady who was with him, and both hastily went inside the room, and the door of the balcony was immediately closed.

"Phoebus!" she cried wildly, "you are alive!" and she fell to the ground, senseless.

Till this time, no one had observed a

He held up the young girl above his head and shouted—"Sanctuary! Sanctuary."

spectator in the gallery above the porch. He was watching all that happened and was so motionless, that he might have been taken for one of those stone monsters of the cathedral. Unobserved, he had tied a knotted rope to one of the small pillars of the gallery, the other end of which reached the pavement. This work done, he had then watched the proceeding as quietly as before.

When the Bohemian girl fainted and he saw the officers coming to lift her, he suddenly strode across the balustrade of the gallery, seized the rope with his knees, feet, and hands and glided down to the pavement. He then swiftly ran up to the two officers, hit both of them with his enormous fists, lifted the Egyptian on one arm and at one bound he was in the church. He held up the young girl above his head and shouted—"Sanctuary! sanctuary!" All this was done within a few seconds.

"Sanctuary! sanctuary!" repeated the crowd; and Quasimodo's only eye was seen

At that moment Quasimodo was really beautiful.

sparkling with joy at the thundering applause he received.

The executioners and other officers stood

shocked. The cathedral was a place of refuge. Within the walls of Notre-Dame the prisoner was safe. No one dared to cross its boundary.

Quasimodo paused under the great porch. He held the girl over his head; but he carried her with as much care so as not to hurt or disturb her. His one eye looked down upon her and there was a flood of tenderness, pity and grief in it. Then the eye suddenly raised flashing lightning. At this sight the crowd stamped with enthusiasm, for at that moment Quasimodo was really beautiful.

The loud noise brought Esmeralda to her senses. She opened her eyes, looked at Quasimodo and instantly closed them again in horror.

After a few moments of triumph, however, quasimodo retired into the interior of church. The people still applauding and shouting, followed him with their eyes.

Chapter 11

THE GHOST

Claude Frollo was no longer in Notre-Dame, when the hunchback saved La Esmeralda from the fatal noose. He had hurried out of the church from a private door and went across the river by a boat and wandered among the hilly streets of the Universite. He did not know where he was, what he did, whether he was awake or dreaming.

At last, on a desert out of the city, he stopped. He thought of the unhappy girl whom he had sent to death. She haunted his every thought. But he did not regret anything. He would rather see her in the hands of the hangman than in the arms of the Captain. But then, the moment he had lost all hope

He thought of the unhappy girl whom he had sent to her death.

of saving the Egyptian, he found that he was almost mad.

"I cannot believe that such a thing could have happened here today."

At nightfall, the confused mind of the Archdeacon began to think of returning. He took a lonely path and reached the bank of the river. There, he found a boatman who took him up the Seine to the point of the Cite, and set him ashore. Claude Frollo remained standing stupidly upon the land, looking straight ahead.

Suddenly he began to run towards Notre-Dame. He saw its enormous towers, lifting themselves in the dark above the houses. When he reached the Place du Parvis, he paused, but dared not raise his eyes towards the parch.

"Oh," he muttered in a low tone. "I cannot believe that such a thing could have happened here today."

The great door of the church was closed, but the Archdeacon always carried with him the key of the tower on which he had his private room. By that door he entered the church and found the interior very dark and quiet.

He slowly started to climb the staircase

He would have fled but was unable to do so.

of the tower, filled with a secret fear. Upon reaching the uppermost gallery, he felt a cool air upon his face. The night was cold and the sky was filled with clouds. The moon gave a very faint light. He cast down his eyes to see the vast city of Paris through a veil of mist and smoke.

At this moment the clock struck twelve. It was midnight. The priest again thought of the girl, who was there twelve hours ago. Suddenly, he saw something white—a human form, a female, appearing at the opposite corner of the tower. By the side of this female, there was a little goat. He shuddered. It was she herself. He would have fled, but was unable to do so. He retreated step by step, till he was beneath the dark side of the staircase.

She walked slowly, almost near the door of the staircase, where she paused for a few moments. She cast a fixed look into the darkness and passed on.

When she was gone, he began to descend the stairs slowly. Horror-sticken, his hair erect, he was convinced that he was in hell itself.

Chapter 12

THE SANCTUARY

In the Middle Ages, the palaces of the King, the churches, had the right of sanctuary. Once a criminal had set foot in the sanctuary he was sacred. These sanctuaries were kind of islands, and considered above the level of human justice. But one step out of this island, he was again captured by the guards, who were always on the watch.

At Notre-Dame it was small cell on the top of the aisle, where Quasimodo had kept La Esmeralda.

When the bell ringer laid her down in the cell of the sanctuary, she felt his huge hands gently loosing the cords that bound her

"Why did you save me?"

arms. She slowly opened her eyes and saw that she was in a church. She recollected having been snatched away from that fatal

The poor fellow was absolutely hideous.

cart, that Phoebus was alive and that he no longer loved her. She then turned towards Quasimodo, who was still standing beside her and said: "Why did you save me?"

He looked anxiously at her, trying to guess what she said. She repeated the question. He slowly withdrew looking very sad. After a few moments he returned, bringing a bundle, which he laid at her feet. It contained a white dress. He went back again and brought a basket and a mattress. The basket contained a bottle, bread and other eatables.

"Eat" said he, setting down the basket. He spread the mattress on the floor, and said, "Sleep."

The girl lifted her eyes to his face to thank him, but could not utter a word. The poor follow was absolutely hideous.

"Ah" said he, "I frighten you, I see. Do not look at me. Stay here in the day time and at night you can walk about all over the church. But do not step out, or they will catch you and kill you."

"Oh Djali, atleast you are not ungrateful."

Moved by his kindness, she raised her head to reply, but he was gone. She was struck by the tone of the voice of his monster, so harsh and so gentle at the same time.

Suddenly she felt the hairy, shaggy head of Djali, brushing against her hands. The girl hugged the goat fondly, which had also escaped in the confusion.

"Oh Djali" she said, "I had almost forgotten you and how you remember me. At least you are not ungrateful."

Evening came on. It was a beautiful night, with soft moonlight. She ventured to take a walk in the high gallery which ran round the church. She felt somewhat refreshed from the walk. It was then that the priest saw her and mistook her for a ghost.

Next morning, when she opened her eyes, she saw the ugly face of Quasimodo in the door of her cell. She involuntarily closed her eyes. But then she heard a hoarse voice saying kindly : "Don't be afraid. I am your friend. I just came to see you sleep. There now, I am behind the wall, you can open your eyes."

When Esmeralda opened her eyes, he was actually no longer there. She went to the window and looked out and saw the poor hunchback covering under the wall. She made an effort to overcome the feeling of aversion.

"Come" she said to him kindly. He started to move away, thinking that she was asking him to go.

She then came out of the cell and ran to him, and took hold of his arm. Quasimodo trembled all over. When he saw that she drew him towards her, his face sparkled with joy and tenderness. But he insisted on staying on the threshold of her cell. "No, no" said he, "the owl never enters the nest of the lark. You must know, I am deaf," he continued, "It is terrible, is to not? While you-you are so beautiful."

"Tell me why you have saved me?" she asked and he read her lips.

"I understand" he said, "you ask me why I saved you. You have forgotten the brute, who attempted one night to carry you off, the one to whom, the very next day you gave water to the pillory. You have forgotten, but I have not."

She listened to him attentively. A tear started to fall from the eye of the bell ringer but he tried to repress it.

"Look," he continued, "we have very high towers here. When you wish to get rid of me, I will throw myself from the top." He then rose to go. Feeling pity for him, she made a sign to stay.

"No, no" said he, "it is out of pity that you do not look away from me. I must not stay too long."

Time passed on; Esmeralda experienced security in the sanctuary. Along with security,

"You have forgotten but I have not."

hope began to revive within her. She often thought of Captain Phoebus. She still believed that Phoebus loved her. So she hoped to meet him again.

The majestic cathedral soothed her broken spirit. Her face recovered its beauty. Her former cheerfulness, her singing, her fondness for her goat returned.

She sometimes thought of Quasimodo. He was the only link she had with the outside world. She did not know what to make of her strange friend, the poor bell-ringer. He often looked in from time to time, to bring provisions for her. But when he saw the look of aversion on her face, he sorrowfully went away.

One morning, Esmeralda was standing on the roof, looking at the Place. Quasimodo was behind her. Suddenly leaning forward she screamed and started waving her hands. "Phoebus! Phoebus!" she cried. Her attitude, her face old Quasimodo that she was in distress. Bending forward, he saw that a handsome young officer was passing the Place on horseback. He was far away to hear the cries of the girl.

Suddenly leaning forward she screamed and started waving her hands.

The poor deaf hunchback understood everything. He signed and said in a low tone,

"That is how one should look from outside." She had meanwhile sunk on her knees and was crying. The hunchback watched her. The poor fellow's eye filled with tears, but he did not allow them to escape. He then gently pulled her sleeve. She turned around.

"Shall I go and fetch him?" he asked quietly.

She cried out in joy. "Oh! go! go, run! that captain!....bring him to me!" she clasped his hands.

Shaking his head sorrowfully, he said; "I will bring him to you" and went down the staircase.

When he reached the Place, there was nobody around except the Captain's horse, fastened to the gate of the mansion which the Captain had entered. Quasimodo looked up to the roof of the church, La Esmeralda was still at the same place. He made a sign to her and leaned against one of the pillars

"Shall I go and fetch him?" he asked quietly.

of the porch, waiting for the captain to come out.

Some hours passed thus, and then night

arrived. Soon afterwards Quasimodo saw the handsome Captain, wrapped in his cloak, passing swiftly before him. Quasimodo ran after him crying "Captain! Captain!"

The Captain stopped his horse and turned to look.

Quasimodo, coming up to him, boldly held his horse.

"Follow me, Captain" said he. "Someone is waiting to speak with you."

"Good heavens" cried the captain, "Let go of my horse scoundrel"

Quasimodo was trying to turn the horse in the opposite direction, unable to understand the Captain's anger.

"Come, Captain" he tried to explain, "It is a girl who is waiting for you- a girl who loves you."

"Tell her, whoever she is" growled the Captain "that I am going to be married, and that she can go to the devil."

Quasimodo boldly held his horse.

"It is the Egyptian, Captain" cried Quasimodo. This made the Captain stop and look at the hunchback again. He thought that this ugly person might have come from hell itself. The street was lonely and his horse was snorting at the sight of Quasimodo.

Suddenly Phoebus hit him with his whip. "Go away" he cried and made his horse run. In an instant he was out of sight of the hunchback.

Sighing deeply, he returned to Notre-Dame and ascended the tower. As he expected, the Bohemian was still at the same place.

"I could not meet him" said he.

"You should have waited all night," she replied angrily.

"I will watch him better another time" he said hanging his head.

From that day he avoided her. Her provisions were brought at night when she was asleep. For some days, she had neither seen nor heard Quasimodo.

She saw a shapeless mass lying outside the door.

One night, however, unable to sleep and while thinking about Phoebus, she heard some noise near her cell. Somewhat frightened she rose, and in the moonlight she saw a shapeless mass lying outside the door. It was Quasimodo, asleep upon the stones.

Chapter 13

THE PRIEST AND THE MAN

Meanwhile, the Archdeacon had come to know about the miraculous manner in which Esmeralda had been saved. He shut himself up in his cell in the tower. He attended neither the conferences nor his usual offices. It was said that he was ill.

From the window of his cell, he could see the girl with her goat, sometimes with Quasimodo. He noticed the little attentions of the hunchback, his respectful and submissive behaviour towards the girl. He witnessed a thousand little scenes between the Egyptian and the hunchback which, strangely, made him jealous-jealous towards Quasimodo. Jealously for the handsome Captain was not surprising, but for the ugly

"Nobody shall have her."

hunchback, it was disturbing to him.

"Nobody shall have her" he used to mutter to himself.

The Archdeacon took Gringoire to a secluded place.

Gringoire was still staying with the vagabonds. He had also come to know that his so called wife had taken sanctuary in

Notre-Dame, and he was very happy about it. He often thought about his favourite goat, Djali, but otherwise he had lost interest in the whole affair.

One day while he was roaming about Paris, he was suddenly stopped by a hand. He turned around to find his old friend and master, the Archdeacon. It was a long time since he had met him. He was surprised to find such a change in the priest. He was very pale, his eyes sunk, and his hair all white.

"Come this way" said the priest, "I have something to say to you." The Archdeacon took Gringoire to a secluded place.

"What are you going to do for La Esmeralda" asked the priest, "Isn't she your wife?"

"You seem to be always thinking about her" said Gringoire.

"And what about you?" Dom Claude asked harshly, "Did she not save your life?"

"I can do something for her and for her goat also."

"I heard that she has taken sanctuary in Notre-Dame and she is quite safe there" said Gringoire.

"But then," cried the priest, "She will be seized again, and will be hanged in the Greve. The Parliament has just issued an order. You have to do something for her."

"Oh Yes," cried Gringoire, "I can do something for her and for her goat also."

"What is it then?" asked the priest impatiently.

"You see," Gringoire began, "she is a favorite with the vagabonds and gipsies. One word to them and they will be ready to do anything for her. Yes" he continued excitedly, "Tomorrow night, they will suddenly attack the cathedral, and in the confusion carry her away. And, by the way, is the little goat still with the girl?"

"Oh, Yes! you scoundrel! just tell me how you will take her away?"

Gringoire bent his lips to the Archdeacon's ear and whispered very softly, casting an

"We shall start in an hour."

uneasy look on the street. When he finished, Dom Claude grasped his hand and said, "Good, tomorrow then?"

"Tomorrow," said Gringoire and they went their own ways.

There was a louder noise than usual in the bar where the vagabonds used to drink. There was more drinking and swearing in the open space where several groups were conversing among each other.

"Come, fellows, hurry" cried Clopin Troullefou, the beggar, "Arm yourselves! We shall start in an hour."

At midnight, Cour des Miracles was dark. Not a single light was to be seen. But the place was filled with people bustling here and there.

"Midnight!" cried Clopin mounting a huge stone. "To your ranks, fellows. Now silence while passing through the streets! No light! until we reach at Notre-Dame! March!"

Within ten minutes the long dark procession started along the winding streets of Paris.

On the same night Quasimodo could not sleep. He had just done his last round in the church. He then went up to the top of the northern tower and there, placing his lantern beside him, began to survey Paris.

A strange feeling of apprehension and uneasiness was upon him, when he looked over the great span of darkness around him.

Suddenly, he noticed that the darkness at the end of a far away street was not still like any other street. It was a moving darkness. Some time passed and then it was clear to him that a crowd of men was coming towards Notre-Dame.

The sight was alarming. Though Quasimodo heard absolutely nothing, he had a confused notion of some impending disaster. For a moment he could not decide what to do. How to save the Egyptian? How to help her to escape? The streets were full of her enemies. There was the river at the back of the church, but no boat! He had only one way—to die at the gate of Notre-Dame in order to save Esmeralda; and not to disturb her sleep until the last moment. This decision once taken, he began to plan his defence. Once again he looked out.

The crowd seemed to be increasing every moment in the Parvis. Suddenly some lighted torches rose above the heads of the crowd. Then Quasimodo could distinctly see the pikes, pickaxes and knives in the hands of the ragged men.

A man appeared to be arranging them and they took their stations about the church.

In the cities and towns of Middle Age, there was no police as such, neither was there any central regulating power to keep control on activities such as this. It was common to attack a palace, or a house in the city without any interference of neighbours.

Suddenly some lighted torches rose above the heads of the crowd.

Some churches were fortified, but unfortunately Notre-Dame was not one of them.

So, as soon as the first arrangements were made, all the vagabonds and beggars stood waiting to hear Clopin's orders. The assembled men were now discussing the ways to rescue their sister—the Egyptian—but unluckly Quasimodo could not hear those words.

"Forward, my boys! To your business!" There was loud cry from Clopin. Thirty stout men sprang from the ranks. They ran towards the great door of the church and began attempting to open it by their levers and other instruments. The door, however, did not move. A crowd of vagabonds rushed to assist, and the eleven steps of the church were filled with people.

Suddenly there was a tremendous crash. An enourmous beam had fallen from the sky and crushed a dozen of the vagabonds on the steps of the church, and bounced down on the pavement with a loud bang. For some

"Forward, my boys!"

seconds the crowd stood staring up at the sky. Nothing could be seen on the top of the tower. The first panic over, they thought of a novel idea; that the very beam could used to ram at the great door.

At once the beam was lifted by two hundred strong arms and it was dashed against the door. At the shock of the beam the immense door resounded like a huge drum. The whole cathedral shook. At the same instant, a shower of stones began to rain upon the crowd. Already a large heap of killed and wounded had collected on the pavement. But the long beam continued at regular intervals inspite of stones.

For Quasimodo, above the tower, there was no time to be lost. He knew that some rooms were full of materials of workmen who had been at work whole day. He had piled all this material—stones, lead, beams, heaps of gravel, where he had stationed himself. There he was then, stooping and rising, stooping and rising again with a superhuman strength.

A shower of stones began to rain on the crowd.

Meanwhile, the panels of the door were cracking, the carving flew off and the wooden plank began to start. Quasimodo knew that the door could not hold out long. Though he could not hear it, he could feel every bang through reverberations.

The men had now crowded around the great door, awaiting impatiently the last grand blow. They were thinking more of the treasures collected in the cathedral for three centuries. They were robbers, and La Esmeralda's rescue was only a pretext for most of them.

All of a sudden a great howl, more hideous than before, burst from the crowd. Those who were not crying and yet alive looked up and saw two streams of molten lead pouring from top of the building. All round these two streams there was a horrible shower of fire.

There was a huge fire on the space between the two towers and below this fire, two statues in the shape of the jaws of

Two streams of molten lead were pouring from the top of the building.

monsters, vomitted those streams of molten lead. All the monstrous statues appeared to have come alive, puffing fire. And one monster was moving from place to place.

"Oh God! It is that horrible bell-ringer!" exclaimed one of the vagabonds. "I know him."

"But let us make one more attempt to go in" said their leader, Clopin. "If not by the door, by a ladder."

In an instant, a ladder that was lying on the pavement was raised and placed against the balustrade of the lower gallery. A bunch of men started climbing up towards the first gallery of the cathedral. But before they could set foot on the gallery, the formidable hunchback sprang on top of the ladder and pushed them from the wall with superhuman force. The long ladder, bending under the heavy load, stood upright for a moment, and then suddenly took a tremendous plunge. An immense noise followed and then all was silent.

"Revenge!" shouted Clopin. "Charge! Charge!

A cry of horror burst from the vagabonds, "Revenge! shouted Clopin, "Charge! charge!"

As Quasimodo watched with concern, a

fearful sea of men rushed towards Notre-Dame by means of some more ladders, knotted ropes or just by holding each other's rags. They were now closing in upon Quasimodo.

Meanwhile the Place was now lighted up with thousands of torches. The fire on the upper platform was still burning and illuminating the city.

Distant alarm-bells had now started ringing. The vagabonds were shouting, swearing and climbing. Quasimodo was now powerless against such a multitude. The brave hunchback, however, had not lost hope to save the Bohemian. He never once thought about his own safety.

Suddenly, there was a tramping of horses in neighbouring streets and then Quasimodo saw a wide line of horsemen advancing towards Notre-Dame like a hurricane. At the head of this line he recognised Captain Phoebus.

"France! France! Forever! Down with the rascals."

"France! France! forever! Down with the rascals!" The cries rang out from the cavalry as they started assaulting the vagabonds.

The conflict was terrible. The Parvis was filled with a dense smoke. The facade of Notre-Dame was faintly seen through this smoke. The vagabonds were taken by surprise. They had no proper weapons and could not take the furious onslaught of the King's troops. They fled in all directions, leaving the Parvis scattered with the dead and wounded.

When Quasimodo watched their defeat, he fell on his knees and lifted his hands to thank heaven. He then ran towards the little cell to see her, whom he had saved so bravely for the second time. When he reached the cell he found it empty.

When the vagabonds attacked the church, La Esmeralda was asleep. But soon, she sat up looking about and listening to the uproar. She then went out of her cell to see what was happening. Upon looking at the scene below, she hurried back to her cell and fell upon her

Then she began to pray for the mercy of God.

knees, filled with horror. Then she began to pray, with heavy sobs, for mercy of God.

She remained in this attitude for some

time, anticipating some terrible disaster. Suddenly she heard footsteps close to her. She looked up. Two men had just entered her cell. One of them carried a lantern. She gave a faint shriek.

"Don't be afraid" said a voice," It's me."

She recognised the voice, yet she asked for his name, to which he replied : "Pierre Gringoire."

That name gave her a fresh courage. The little goat, Djali, had already gone up to him to rub her head against his knees.

"Ah, Djali knew me before you did" Gringoire said fondly.

"And who is that with you?" said the girl suspiciously.

"Don't worry" answered Gringoire, "It is one of my friends."

She saw that the man was covered from head to foot, which scared her more.

She saw that the man was covered from head to foot.

"My poor child" resumed Gringoire, "Your life is in danger, and Djali's too. We have come to save you. Come with us."

She had to accept the situation, though she was afraid to accompany the black figure.

Gringoire took her by the hand. His companion picked up the lantern and walked on before them. The goat went with them, jumping with joy upon seeing Gringoire again.

They quickly climbed down the tower stairs, passed through the dark, solitary church which was ringing from the uproar. Gringoire's companion unlocked a door at the back, and they were on the Terrian. The Terrian was a slip of land enclosed with walls, belonging to Notre-Dame. This spot was entirely deserted and the terrible noise was already at some distance.

At the point of the Terrain, at the water's edge, near the decayed fence, a small boat was hidden beneath the tree branches.

The man with the lantern went upto the

The man went upto the boat, made a sign to Gringoire and the girl to get in.

boat and made a sign to Gringoire and the girl to get in. Then the man stepped in himself and cut the rope which moored the boat. Taking up the two oars, he began to now.

The first thing Gringoire did, after getting into the boat, was to take his seat and to lift the goat upon his knees. The girl sat down by Gringoire, pressing close to him, quite afraid of the other man.

The unknown had not uttered a word, as he rowed towards the right bank of the river.

The noise around Notre-Dame had now increased. They listened. Shouts of victory were distinctly heard. Suddenly a hundred torches appeared on all parts of the church—the towers, the galleries, the balustrade. And then shouts of "The Egyptian! the Sorceress! death to the Egyptian!" were clearly heard.

The unlucky girl dropped her head upon her hands. The unknown began to row more furiously towards the shore. Gringoire

The unknown began to row more furiously towards the shore.

hugged the goat in his arms and gently moved away from the Bohemian. He had tears in his eyes when he muttered to himself : "I cannot save both of them."

Suddenly they were near the right bank. The unknown stood up and offered his hand to the Egyptian. When she refused and clung to Gringoire's sleeve, he almost pushed her away. She then jumped on the shore without help and stood still for a moment, fixing her eyes on the water. The poor girl was so alarmed, that she did not know what was happening around her.

Suddenly, after some moments, she realized that she was now alone with the mysterious man, that Gringoire had slipped away with the goat among the cluster of houses. She shuddered and tried to cry out, to call Gringoire, but not a sound came from her lips.

At once the man clasped her hand and with hasty steps, began to move towards the Place de Greve. She followed him mechanically.

The unknown continued to drag her along silently.

The bank at this spot was absolutely deserted. They could only hear the distant cries at Notre-Dame which pronounced her death.

Meanwhile the unknown continued to drag her along silently, holding her tightly. She ceased to resist and followed him helplessly. From time to time she asked in a broken voice, "Who are you?—Who are you?" He did not reply.

At last they stopped at an open space. From the moonlight, she realised it was Greve. There was a black cross in the middle of the Greve—it was the gibbet.

The man turned towards her and raised his hood.

"Oh" she stammered, "I knew it must be him."

It was, in fact the priest. He looked like a ghost in the moonlight.

"Listen to me," he said in a hoarse voice. "This is the Greve. We will go no further. Your life is at my disposal. And now don't say

He pointed towards the gallows, while clasping her tightly with his other hand.

a single word about your Phoebus." He paced to and fro and drew her with him . Then he stood still.

"Listen to me," he continued, "This is a serious business. The Parliament has ordered to put you to death again. I have rescued you from their hands. But they are still searching for you." He pointed towards the Cite. They could hear the noise coming nearer and the cries, "The Egyptian! where is the Egyptian!"

"You can see they are after you" said he. "I love you. I have helped you to escape. You will have to choose between me and the gibbet." He pointed towards the gallows, while clasping her tightly with his other hand.

She tore herself from his clasp and threw herself towards the fatal machine. "This is less horrible than you!" said she, half turning her head to look at the priest.

"I love you" he said again. His tone was now soft and plaintive, "It's a torture! night and day! Tell me, will you never have pity on me? Will you hate me forever? It is this hate which makes me cruel. And yet, you are

The priest clasped her furiously in his arms.

so good, so gentle and charming. Alas! only towards me you do not have any feeling. Oh! How unfortunate!"

He buried his face in his hands. And Esmeralda heard him weep. He was shaking by sobs. He wept like this for some time.

"Oh!" he proceeded, "Do not condemn both of us like this. I am a priest, yet I am disgracing my name—all for your sake. One word! Only one word of kindness! If not love me, say only that you wish me well. It will be enough. I will save you. The time is passing. One kind word! Please!" he begged as he sank on his knees.

She opened her lips to answer. He listened attentively.

"You are a murderer!" said she.

The priest clasped her furiously in his arms : "murderer I may be!" he cried, "But you will be mine. And I will be your master. I will not suffer anymore. You must die or be mine. Decide now."

His eyes sparkled with passion and rage.

"I will see you hanged."

"Oh! You hateful monk!" she cried, "Loose me."

Turning pale, he released her from his

grip. She continued: "I belong to my Phoebus. He is handsome. I love him. As for you, go away you ugly old priest."

He gave a violent cry, "Die then" said he gritting his teeth.

Just then she could hear the sound of many galloping horses very near to them. They were the King's soldier searching their victim.

"I will fetch the sergeants. I will see you hanged" said the priest.

Esmeralda saw the priest running towards Notre-Dame, just as the soldiers on horse-back approached the Greve.

When Quasimodo had made sure that the cell was empty, that the Egyptian was taken, while he was defending the cathedral for her, he grasped his head in both his hands and cried with rage and astonishment.

He then began to run all over the church to find the girl. At that moment the King's

He himself assisted them in this search.

soldiers entered the church, also to seek the Egyptian.

Poor deaf Quasimodo! He himself assisted

them in this search : showed them every possible place of concealment, opened all the secret doors, all the while thinking that they had come to save her, while he had fought with the vagabonds whom he regarded as the girl's enemies.

After a long time, this unsuccessful search was over and the soldiers went out of the church. When he was quite sure that the girl was no longer there, Quasimodo began to ascend the tower-stairs slowly. The church was once more empty and silent. The unhappy hunchback slowly went into the Egyptian's cell. He remained there for a while in a state of shock.

Then he leaned on the girl's bed and gently kissed the place where she used to sleep. He remained thus for sometime as motionless as if dead. Suddenly he rose, and beside himself with rage, dashed his head against the wall again and again. At last he fell exhausted. He then made himself come

He passed on above Quasimodo without noticing him.

out of the cell and crouched opposite to the door. He sat there for almost an hour, without moving, his eye fixed on the vacant cell, like a sad mother who is seated near an empty cradle.

It was then that he began to think about the Archdeacon. He recollected that only the priest had a key to the stair-case leading to the cell. He remembered the Archdeacon's attempt to snatch the girl, in which, he Quasimodo himself had assisted. He was convinced then that the priest had taken the girl from him. But such was his respect towards the priest, that even at this moment he could not feel jealous towards him. It only increased his grief.

At this moment, as dawn began to whiten the cathedral, he noticed a figure going rapidly towards the north tower. It was the Archdeacon. He was trying to see something across the right bank of the Seine. He passed on above Quasimodo without noticing him. The hunchback rose and followed the Archdeacon, to see what he was now up to.

He only followed the direction of the priest's gaze.

When he had reached the top of the tower, before coming out of the darkness, he cautiously looked about for the priest. The

Archdeacon had his back to him. He was leaning against the corner of the balustrade which is just above the bridge of Notre-Dame. His attention was so completely engrossed that he did not notice the hunchback.

Paris, viewed from the towers of Notre-Dame in the cool dawn was a magnificent sight. The sun was just rising. The sky was serene. The river could be seen with silver lines. Above the towers, in the air, small birds were twittering and singing.

But the priest neither heard nor saw any of these things. He had concentrated at only one point, his eyes fixed on a particular spot. The hunchback dared not disturb him. He only followed the direction of the priest's gaze, and thus his eyes fell upon the Place de Greve.

He could see a ladder was set up against the permanent gibbet. There were many soldiers at the Place. A man was dragging

"Damnation!" cried the priest as he fell.

along the pavement someone in white. He then began to mount the ladder. Quasimodo could clearly see that he carried a woman across his shoulder, a young woman, dressed in white, and a rope around her neck. Quasimodo instantly recognized Esmeralda.

The man now reached the top of the ladder, and arranged the rope. The priest now knelt down upon the balustrade in order to see more clearly.

The man suddenly kicked away the ladder and Quasimodo saw the unfortunate girl dangling at the end of the rope.

At this most crucial moment, a terrible laugh, a laugh which was no longer human, burst forth from the priest. Quasimodo did not hear but saw this laugh and recoiled a few steps back from the priest. Then suddenly rushing furiously upon him, he thrust him with his huge hands into the abyss.

"Damnation!" cried the priest as he fell.

The gutter beneath caught him and broke the fall. He clung to it, and just when he was about to cry for help, he saw the savage face

The leaden pipe began to bend with his weight.

of Quasimodo over the balustrade. Then he did not utter a word.

The abyss was beneath him—a fall of

more than two hundred feet—and the pavement! The priest made great efforts to come on the edge of the gutter. But the hands had not hold on the granite. His efforts were fruitless.

Quasimodo might have withdrawn him by merely reaching him his hand, but he did not even look at him. He was looking at the Egyptian; never turning his eye from the only object which existed for him at that moment. A stream of tears flowed silently from that eye.

The Archdeacon meanwhile began to pant. Blood oozed from his finger's ends; the skin was rubbed from his knees against the wall. The leaden pipe where the gutter ended, began to bend with his weight. The priest felt it slowly giving way. The horror of the fall thrilled his bones. At times he wildly looked about himself. Once he glanced at the abyss beneath him and closed his eyes. His hair stood erect.

The grip loosened and down he fell!

When the Archdeacon was experiencing the most horrible agonies of death, Quasimodo kept his eye fixed on the Greve and wept. There was something frightening in the silence of these two persons.

There was the Archdeacon, now determined not to move. He was scarcely breathing and his fixed eyes glared a wild and ghastly manner. He felt his arms becoming weaker and weaker and the laden pipe which supported him bent more and more.

Once again, the Archdeacon, foaming with rage and terror, tried to muster all this remaining strength for a last effort. He succeeded in raising himself about a foot, setting both his knees against the wall. But this struggle caused the leaden pipe to give way suddenly. Feeling himself sinking, the wretched man closed his eyes. The grip loosened and down he fell!

Quasimodo watched him falling—sliding rapidly down the roof, down the went and rebounded on the pavement. He then stirred no more.

Two skeletons were found in a peculiar posture.

Quasimodo then again looked at the Egyptian, dangling from the gallows. He then looked at the Archdeacon, stretched at the foot of the tower, and sighing deeply, he cried, "There is all I ever loved!"

In the evening of the same day, when the Bishop's officers came to remove the corpse of the Archdeacon from the pavement, Quasimodo was nowhere to be seen.

According to the general rumour, Quasimodo, the devil, was to carry away Calude Frollo, the sorcerer.

He was never seen afterwards and it was never known what became of him.

On the following night of La Esmeralda's execution, her body was removed from the gibbet, and according to custom, was taken to the vault of Montfaucon.

Montfaucon was the most ancient gallow in the kingdom of France. The hollow stone-work had served to form a vast vault, into which were thrown the bodies of the executed at the permanent gibbets of Paris.

About a year and a half after the execution of La Esmeralda, when a search was made in the vault of Montfaucon, for the body of some other person, among these carcases two skeletons were found in a peculiar posture. One of these was of the woman. It had still upon it, some fragments of a white dress. The other, which had embraced the first one, was that of a man. The spine of his skeleton was crooked, the head depressed in the shoulders, and the legs bowed. It was evident that this person had not been hanged. He must have come here and died. When they attempted to disengage this skeleton from its grasp, it crumbled to dust.